T0030306

Who Is
Michael Phelps?

by Micah Hecht

illustrated by Manuel Gutierrez

Penguin Workshop

For all the neurodivergent kids who've ever felt
most at home in the water—MH

To Michael and his family—MG

PENGUIN WORKSHOP
An imprint of Penguin Random House LLC, New York

First published in the United States of America by Penguin Workshop,
an imprint of Penguin Random House LLC, New York, 2024

Visit us online at penguinrandomhouse.com.

Library of Congress Cataloging-in-Publication Data is available.

Printed in the United States of America

ISBN 9781524791025 (paperback)   10 9 8 7 6 5 4 3 2 1 WOR
ISBN 9781524791032 (library binding)   10 9 8 7 6 5 4 3 2 1 WOR

Contents

Who Is Michael Phelps?

On August 15, 2008, the world's eyes were on one man in a swimming pool in Beijing, China. Every day of the 2008 Summer Olympics had been filled with excitement. But today, an American swimmer from Maryland was taking a step to become one of the greatest athletes in history.

Michael Phelps, who was twenty-three years old, stood behind lane five of the swimming pool. Reporters and athletes called the building the "Water Cube" because its walls and ceiling were made of glass panels that looked like bubbles. The view of the ceiling made you feel like you were underwater! So far that week, Michael had swum six other Olympic final races. He had finished each of those races faster than the other swimmers, taking home six gold medals. If he could win seven gold medals, he would tie former professional swimmer Mark Spitz as the athlete to win the most gold medals in one Olympics. If he could win eight gold medals, he would do something no one had ever done before!

Michael stepped onto the starting block. He bent at the hips, raised his arms back behind him, and let them fall down. His arms crossed his chest with a great slapping sound. That was his signature move. It was how Michael warmed up his muscles and let the competition know who they were up against. The arm-clap sound rang out once, twice, three times throughout the Water Cube.

"Take your marks."

Michael took a step forward with his left foot and gripped his hands on the edge of the starting block. *Beep!* The starting sound rang out. The swimmers dove into the pool. Michael could hear water whooshing by his ears. His arms were tight against his head in a streamlined dive position. He dolphin kicked to the surface. Then he started to swim the butterfly stroke. Both arms came up and over the water together, then dove back in to pull him forward.

A swimmer from Serbia was in the lane next to Michael. Before the race, the swimmer had told reporters that he wanted to beat Michael.

"It would be nice if historians talk about Michael Phelps winning seven gold medals and losing the eighth to some guy. I'd like to be that guy," the other swimmer had said.

Hearing this before the race made Michael want to win even more.

The race was the 100-meter butterfly. At the halfway mark, Michael saw his competitor was well ahead of him. Michael picked up speed through the second half. In the final two meters, he could see the other swimmer gliding into the wall. The other swimmer's arms extended just inches from the end of the pool. In that split second, Michael had a decision to make: He could glide into the wall and finish second. Or he could take an extra half stroke and see if it could get him to the finish faster. Even the youngest swimmers can tell you that half strokes into the finish are usually too slow. But this was a special case.

To keep his dream alive, Michael brought his arms over his head one last time and touched the wall. He turned and looked at the scoreboard. Surely, he had lost the race.

1. Michael Phelps USA: 50.58
2. Milorad Cavic SRB: 50.59

Michael (left) wins the 100-meter butterfly final, 2008 Summer Olympics

He had won his seventh Olympic gold of the 2008 Summer Olympics by the smallest possible margin! He was now on his way to becoming the greatest Olympic athlete of all time!

CHAPTER 1
A Boy Full of Energy

Michael Fred Phelps II was born on June 30, 1985, in Baltimore, Maryland. As a young child, Michael lived with his mother, father, and two older sisters in Towson, Maryland. His mother, Debbie, was a middle-school principal. His father, also named Michael but who was known as Fred, was a police officer.

As a kid, Michael loved causing mischief. If a parent or teacher told him not to do something, he had to try it! Michael wasn't afraid to eat a big spoonful of spicy hot sauce, and he would play with his food, mixing it all together on his plate and pouring milk on top to make a soup.

Sitting still was the hardest thing for Michael to do. He always wanted to keep moving or fidgeting. His body just felt better when it was moving. Michael liked to twirl pens and pencils in between his middle fingers. Sometimes pens and pencils weren't available, so he would try twirling whatever he could find! He loved climbing on things that were not meant for climbing.

He made funny faces whenever someone tried to take a picture of him. He wrestled with his friends. When adults asked him questions, he would answer with his own questions.

It wasn't until Michael was nine years old that his mom took him to the doctor to figure out if they could help him. After speaking with Michael, a doctor diagnosed him with attention deficit hyperactivity disorder (ADHD). This is a medical condition that makes it difficult for some people to stay focused on a task or sit still. Today, kids and adults with ADHD can talk about the positive ways it affects their lives and personalities. They say that having ADHD is not good or bad. It's just different.

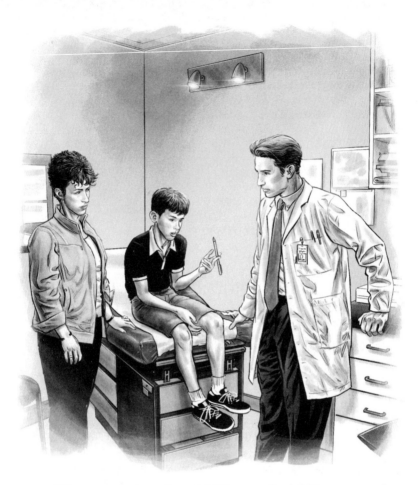

However, in the 1980s and 1990s, people were more likely to think of ADHD as a bad thing. They thought there was only one "right" kind of brain. Some of Michael's classmates and teachers were supportive of his uniqueness.

His third-grade teacher told him that he had "an active personality." She thought his fidgeting was healthy. Instead of telling Michael what to do, she asked him what *he* wanted to do. But many adults and classmates in Michael's life were not very kind to him because of his fidgeting. One elementary school teacher told Michael's mom, "I just don't ever see him being able to focus on anything in his life."

Attention Deficit Hyperactivity Disorder (ADHD)

Many kids sometimes have trouble sitting still, being patient, or listening. But children with ADHD deal with these issues all the time.

People with ADHD may also have boundless energy. Or they might have the ability to focus extra hard on the things they love. Or they may be very creative or courageous. Some people see ADHD as a disorder, like a disease. But more and more people with ADHD are starting to say that they do not have a disorder, they are just different.

Daily life can still be a struggle, though, for people with ADHD. Many schools, public places, and workplaces aren't set up for people whose brains work differently. Sometimes medications can help kids and adults with ADHD focus more easily.

Michael would also get picked on by bullies who would make fun of the way he spoke with a lisp or the size of his ears. Some kids would flick his ears or call him "Spock"—a pointy-

eared character from the television show *Star Trek*. Michael liked to wear hats to cover his ears and avoid being made fun of, but sometimes kids would grab his hat and throw it onto the street.

Spock from *Star Trek*

When Michael was in elementary school, two things happened that changed his life forever: He started swimming, and his parents got divorced. In 1994, Michael's parents made the decision to end their marriage, and Michael's father moved out of their family home. Michael couldn't believe it. The divorce didn't feel real for him until days later.

Usually, Michael had to wait hours for his dad to be done with the computer so that he could play games. But one day after his dad moved out, Michael went to the computer and realized he didn't have to wait anymore. His dad wasn't coming back. Swimming was one way Michael dealt with his feelings about his parents' divorce.

Years earlier, a doctor had told Debbie that children should learn how to swim for water safety, so she enrolled Michael's older sisters, Hilary and Whitney, for swim lessons, and they later joined the swim team. Michael would hear their alarms going off at 4:00 a.m. for morning swim practice. Hilary and Whitney both became very accomplished swimmers.

Michael and his sisters, late 1980s

When Michael was seven years old, it was his turn to get into the pool. Debbie decided that swimming might also be a good way for Michael to work off some of his boundless energy. At his first lesson, he hated the water. He was scared to get his face wet. He kicked and screamed. When that didn't work, he asked to stop, saying he was tired and cold. "That's your problem, Michael

Phelps," his swimming teacher said. "Your mom wants you to learn how to swim, so you're going to swim."

His teacher started off by teaching Michael how to float on his back. At least when he floated on his back, the water wasn't in his face. After a few lessons, Michael started to get better at swimming. Then it wasn't as scary to flip over and put his face into the water. Soon, he wanted to spend every free moment in the pool.

CHAPTER 2
Into the Pool

Michael joined his sisters on the North Baltimore Aquatic Club swim team. It was soon clear that swimming helped him learn and grow in a way that school couldn't.

Michael had struggled with math all his life. But Debbie was amazed when he started talking to her about fractions and decimals. He could explain how 0.1 second could make a big difference in a swimming race. Michael started calculating swimming distances by adding three- and four-digit numbers in his head. If only his math teacher could relate all his math problems to swimming!

When he was eight, Michael started winning swimming races. He got fast enough to join a more serious training group with older kids. At the time, Michael knew he was winning most of his races against other eight-year-olds. He did not know, however, that he was one of the fastest eight-year-olds in the entire United States!

One of Michael's best strokes was the butterfly. Swimmers lie on their stomachs and move both of their arms over the water at the same time. Both of their legs do a "dolphin" kick, moving up and down at the same time. Butterfly is the stroke many kids and adults find the most difficult. But Michael's arms were very long for a kid his age. His long arms and unlimited energy helped him maintain a perfect technique and remain focused for a full race.

Other kids were no match for him.

Michael was very emotional as a young swimmer. He was hard on himself when he couldn't meet his goals. Sometimes he would cry or get angry when a race didn't go his way. After finishing a race and seeing that he didn't win, Michael would get mad and throw his goggles across the pool deck.

The Four Strokes

There are four strokes in competitive swimming: butterfly, backstroke, breaststroke, and freestyle.

Butterfly is swum on the stomach, where the swimmer's arms move over the water at the same time and their legs also move up and down at the same time. Backstroke is swum on the back. Swimmers look up at the sky or ceiling. Arms move alternately in a "windmill" motion. Legs move in a "flutter" kick, alternating up and down very fast.

Butterfly

Backstroke

Breaststroke is swum on the stomach. Arms stay under the water, moving in an upside down "heart" motion. Legs move in a "frog" kick. Freestyle is the fastest stroke. It is sometimes called the "front crawl" or "Australian crawl." Freestyle is swum on the stomach. Arms alternate in a circle pattern. Legs move in a "flutter" kick, alternating up and down very fast.

The medley is a swimming event where participants swim all four strokes in a particular order. Medleys can be swum by one swimmer: an individual medley, called an IM. They can also be swum by four swimmers each swimming one stroke: a medley relay.

Breaststroke

Freestyle

In one swim meet, when Michael was ten years old, he finished second in the 200-yard freestyle. He lost the race to another kid his age. He felt the anger boiling up. But then he decided not to release the anger by throwing his goggles. Instead, he chose to take the anger and use it to help him prepare for his next races. By doing this, he won each of the next five races! In all five, he broke the record for the fastest American swimmer in the nine- or ten-year-old category.

After that, Michael learned there were other ways to work through his emotions. Whenever he felt angry, he used the anger as motivation. He was becoming one of the best elementary-school swimmers in the country. Meanwhile, his fourteen-year-old sister, Whitney, was becoming one of the best swimmers in the country of any age. She had recently won a national title in the 200-meter butterfly race. Michael would overhear people saying that

Whitney was going to be the next star in United States swimming.

But something very sad happened: Whitney had been keeping a secret. She had hurt her back during one of her practice lessons, and the injury affected how she swam. She went to the 1996 Olympic trials—a competition to see which athletes would qualify for the Summer Olympics—but she did not do well and wasn't chosen for the US team. The Summer Olympics is the most important event for swimmers, and they only happen every four years. After going to the doctor, Whitney learned she would not be able to swim competitively again. This injury not only caused Whitney physical pain but also mental pain. She was not motivated to do anything and hardly spoke with her friends and family. Michael felt bad for his sister, but he also learned that he needed to speak up if he was ever in pain.

Around that time, Michael moved up to an advanced group of swimmers on his team. He was the only eleven-year-old training with a crew of fast thirteen- and fourteen-year-olds.

Moving up also meant that Michael started working with a new coach: Bob Bowman. Michael thought Bob was very intimidating. He seemed to have eyes in the back of his head. Whether Michael was sneakily skipping laps,

Bob Bowman

arriving late, splashing his teammates, or playing pranks, Bob always knew exactly what Michael had done. At first, Bob and Michael seemed like opposites who would never work well together. Bob was very organized and logical. Michael, on the other hand, was a goofball with lots of energy.

The Summer Olympics

The Summer Olympic Games are a multisport international competition that takes place every four years. The first version of the Olympic Games was held across ancient Greece from the 700s BC to the AD 300s. They were a series of athletic competitions like boxing, running, and chariot racing in honor of the ancient Greek god Zeus. The modern Olympic Games were first held in 1896 in Athens, Greece. The competition is always held in a different city.

Every Olympic event awards three medals: gold for first place, silver for second place, and bronze for third place. The Olympic Games—both Summer and Winter—are incredibly popular. Many people who don't usually watch sports watch the Olympic Games on television because the games bring together the world's most talented athletes to see who is the best. Many of the athletes become international celebrities.

Besides swimming, other Summer Olympics events include gymnastics, cycling, fencing, and archery.

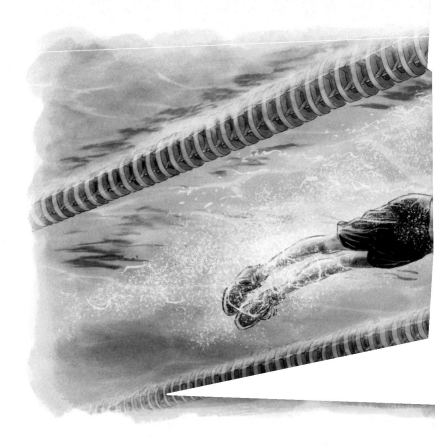

But working with Bob had a big effect on Michael's swimming performance. Bob liked to keep workouts creative. Sometimes he had Michael practice swimming with arms only, legs only, or one arm and one leg. Sometimes Bob would have Michael swim in sneakers!

Or with a floating tube around his ankles! Or he would make Michael swim without goggles. These creative workouts would always teach Michael something about proper technique. Or they would teach him how to keep calm in a high-pressure situation. Or how to make up for a swimming mistake, like accidentally breaking your goggles.

When Michael was twelve years old, Bob called both Debbie and Michael's father, Fred, in for a meeting. Bob told them Michael could become a very successful swimmer one day. Maybe he could even compete in the Olympics! However, Bob was very careful not to put too much pressure on Michael or make him feel overwhelmed. Bob even made a rule that no one on the team could say the word *Olympics* around Michael.

CHAPTER 3
Olympic Rings

When Michael was fourteen and going into high school, he faced a big choice. In the past, he had juggled swimming with other sports, including baseball and lacrosse. When his friends signed up for the high-school golf and football teams, Michael wanted to join, too. But his swimming commitments had increased over the years. He had practice nearly every day, sometimes both in the morning and at night. And swim meets were held almost every weekend. After talking it over with his mom, Michael decided swimming would have to become his only sport.

In March 2000, Michael competed in the United States Spring National Championships.

This was a big competition where participants swim two races for each event: a preliminary and a final race. During the preliminary event, Michael swam faster than any thirteen- to sixteen-year-old in US history.

After that race, Bob took a walk by himself in the parking lot. He told himself, "Michael's going to make the Olympic team. . . . The 2000 Olympic team. I better get him ready." That night in the final, Michael finished third in a race between the best teenagers and adults in the country! *Swimming World* magazine wrote: "Fourteen-year-old Michael Phelps swam a phenomenal 1:59.02 at spring nationals, but is probably a year or two away from being a factor on the world scene."

Bob disagreed. Michael was going to turn fifteen in June, right before the 2000 Olympics in Sydney, Australia. No men's swimmer his age had qualified for a US Olympic team since 1932. But Bob thought Michael could do it.

Built for Speed

Even though Michael Phelps trains regularly, his body also seems to be perfectly built for swimming.

He is six feet and four inches tall, but he has a wingspan (distance of outstretched arms) that is six feet and seven inches wide. This means that his long arms let him pull more water than someone with shorter arms. He also has short legs and a long torso. His proportions give him more pull from his chest and arms and more stability in his legs.

Michael also has hypermobile (or double-jointed) joints. Paired with his size-fourteen feet, his bendy ankles can act as flippers. Michael has also said that his sense of touch is hypersensitive—that means he can feel how the water flows across his body better than most people can. This helps him adjust his technique to become more efficient in the water.

Researchers have also found that Michael's body creates less lactic acid, a substance that builds up in your muscles and makes you feel tired. This means that he can swim farther and faster without getting tired.

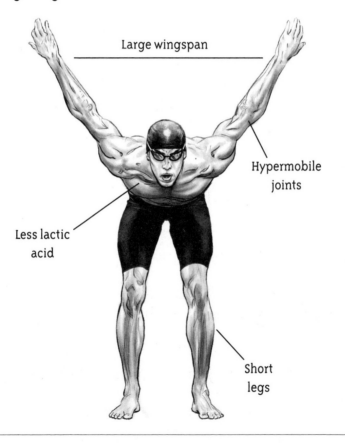

Large wingspan

Hypermobile joints

Less lactic acid

Short legs

It was now Michael's chance to swim in the 2000 Olympic Team Trials, the qualifying competition for the 2000 Summer Olympics. Finishing first or second in an event at the Olympic Trials usually guarantees you a spot on the US Olympic team.

At the meet, Michael easily qualified for the 200-meter butterfly race. In the final, he was the youngest person swimming. The other seven competitors were aged eighteen to twenty-three. And they had been swimming at elite levels for years and years.

But Michael believed in himself and finished second! He had become the youngest swimmer to make the US men's Olympic swim team in nearly seventy years!

A few weeks later, at the Summer Olympics in Sydney, Australia, Michael finished fifth in his race. It was a very good performance. But he did not win a medal.

Michael comes in second place in the 200-meter butterfly, 2000 Summer Olympic Trials.

After the Olympics, most athletes take a break from training to recover. Michael didn't. He jumped into the pool the very next day for practice. At that practice, Bob handed Michael a sheet of paper with his next goal written on it: "WR." WR stood for world record: the fastest time in history in an event. With proper training,

Bob thought Michael could become the fastest swimmer in history in the 200-meter butterfly. Even faster than any adult swimmer in the world had ever been.

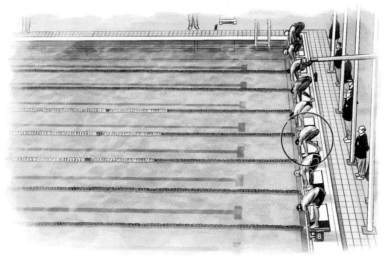

Michael (in lane six) prepares for the 200-meter butterfly event at the 2000 Sydney Olympics.

In the meantime, Michael enjoyed the excitement of being an Olympian. He begged his mom to let him get a tattoo of the Olympic rings. The Olympic rings are the symbol of the Olympic Games. Getting them as a tattoo is a tradition for many Olympic athletes. Eventually, Debbie agreed, and Michael got the tattoo on his hip.

Because of his Olympic performance, fifteen-year-old Michael got to experience many things most people his age only dreamed about. He threw out the first pitch for a Baltimore Orioles baseball game. He got to meet members of his favorite football team, the Baltimore Ravens. He even went to the White House to meet President Bill Clinton.

When he wasn't out meeting new people and making incredible memories, Michael was training. He and Bob had created the goal for Michael to set a world record at a swim meet in Austin, Texas, in the spring. And Michael met that goal. In the spring of 2001, he swam the 200-meter butterfly faster than any swimmer in history. He even beat the Olympic gold medalist!

After the world record, Bob and Michael set many small goals for Michael that would lead up to the 2004 Olympic Games in Athens, Greece, when Michael would be nineteen. Their goals started to expand beyond Michael's main event, the 200-meter butterfly. Michael wanted to focus on becoming one of the best in the world in many different swimming events. Maybe he could even become the best overall swimmer in history.

In 2001, as a junior in high school, Michael signed a sponsorship deal with the swimwear company Speedo. That made him a professional swimmer, someone who gets paid for competing in their sport. Swimming was now Michael's job, and Speedo, along with other companies, paid him to do it.

When Michael was in Sydney for the Olympics and on later trips to Australia, he saw that Australian swimmers were like rock stars in their country. Swimming was the top story in the news. Swimmers were on billboards and in commercials. Each Olympics, the top Australian swimmers would become national heroes. At that time in the United States, swimming was not a very popular sport. Michael was frustrated that historic races in swimming were not covered in the news. He dreamed of seeing swimming highlights on ESPN's *SportsCenter*, a popular television sports program. He wanted kids to look up to the greatest swimmers and to love the sport as much as they loved basketball and football. He wanted to make swimming as big in the United States as it was in Australia.

CHAPTER 4
One Million Dollars?

The 2004 Summer Olympics were going to be an even bigger event than the Olympics usually are because they were returning to their home in Athens, Greece, for the first time since the modern Olympic Games began in 1896.

Michael trained harder than ever. He also graduated from high school. He won national and world championship titles leading up to 2004. As excitement started to build for the Olympics, Michael signed a new agreement with Speedo. If he could win seven gold medals at the 2004 Olympics in Athens or at the 2008 Olympics in Beijing, China, Speedo would pay him a bonus of $1 million! Word of the million-dollar bonus started to spread. It was a huge amount of money, and the deal brought a lot of attention to Michael and to the sport of swimming.

Seven was a significant number. It was the all-time record for the number of gold medals won by a single person in one Olympics. The record was set by swimmer Mark Spitz in 1972.

Mark Spitz

As the Athens Summer Olympics came closer, Michael was becoming more and more famous. He was being interviewed and signing up for more print advertisements and commercials. Michael was featured on the cover of *Sports Illustrated* magazine for the first time. He even appeared in one TV commercial where he raced against a dolphin!

Michael wins the 400-meter individual medley, 2004 Olympics

At the 2004 Olympics, Michael ended up winning six gold medals and two bronze medals. It wasn't enough to win the $1 million. But it was enough to give Michael the second-greatest performance ever at a single Olympics, behind Mark Spitz's 1972 Olympics.

Mark Spitz (1950–)

Born on February 10, 1950, Mark Spitz is widely known as one of the greatest swimmers in history. Mark grew up in California and Hawaii. He learned to swim at age two, and he became the world's best ten-and-under swimmer. His teammates called him "Mark the Shark."

At the 1972 Summer Olympics in Munich, Germany, Mark won seven Olympic gold medals. He also set a new world record in each swimming event. At the time, it made him the greatest Olympian in history. He won more gold medals in a single Olympics than anyone ever had.

Mark was known for his signature mustache. In swimming, most athletes shave all their facial and body hair to reduce drag in the water. (*Drag* is the force that slows people down as they are moving through water.) So it was unique for a swimmer to have a mustache. And it made Spitz very recognizable at the time.

The race that showed Michael's generous character the best, however, was a race he didn't even swim.

Michael's teammate Ian Crocker had been

Ian Crocker

sick during the week of the Olympics. Ian's signature event was the 100-meter butterfly. He and Michael were going to compete against each other. Usually, Ian would have beat Michael, but his illness was slowing him down. The winner of the event would get a gold medal, and he would also get to swim the butterfly in the Olympic finals of the 4 × 100-meter medley relay for the United States. This medley race sees each of the four swimmers on a team swim a 100-meter leg of the relay, each swimming a different stroke in the following order: backstroke, breaststroke, butterfly, and freestyle. It is a big honor to get to swim on the United States relays in the Olympics.

Michael beat Ian to the gold. Ian took the silver medal in the event. Ian was disappointed, not only because he lost the race, but also because it meant that he wouldn't get to swim the relay.

Michael thought long and hard about it. Ian was starting to get over his illness and was feeling better with each passing day. By the time the relay came up, Ian would probably be fast enough to beat the competition. If Michael swam on the relay, Ian was going to leave Athens without an Olympic gold medal.

Michael decided to give his relay spot to Ian. He stood in the stands and watched as Ian and the rest of the relay team won the gold medal in world-record time! Michael cheered for the team's victory, knowing he had done the right thing.

Ian Crocker embraces Michael after Team USA wins the 4 × 100-meter medley relay, 2004

CHAPTER 5
A Chance to Be the Greatest

Once he came back from the 2004 Summer Olympics, Michael experienced a lot of changes. Bob had become more than a coach to Michael: He was also a father figure. Bob was especially important because Michael had a rocky relationship with his own father. Fred hardly ever spent time with his children since his divorce. Bob told Michael he had taken a job as the head swim coach at the University of Michigan. Michael didn't have to think twice about it. He moved to Michigan as well. He didn't pick a major or try to attain a specific degree, but he did enroll in several classes at the university. His main focus was training with Bob. Michael trained for three to five hours a day, seven days a week.

His life during that time was concentrated around eating, sleeping, and swimming. He didn't even take holidays off.

Michael does a photo shoot at the University of Michigan pool.

Michael and Bob broke swimming down to a science. Michael became even more obsessed with numbers. He knew the number of strokes to take in every event on every lap. He knew what it felt like to be 0.1 seconds off his goal in a race. He studied videos of the other top swimmers in the world. He told reporters that he knew some of his opponents' swimming styles better than they did.

Eat Up!

In order to keep his body energized during his intense daily training sessions and swim meets, Michael said he ate about eight thousand to ten thousand calories a day! Here is what Michael might have eaten on a typical day while he was swimming professionally:

- Breakfast: Three fried-egg sandwiches with cheese, lettuce, tomatoes, fried onions, and mayonnaise. Two cups of coffee. One five-egg omelet. One bowl of grain. Three slices of French toast topped with powdered sugar. Three chocolate-chip pancakes.
- Lunch: One pound of pasta. Two large ham-and-cheese sandwiches with mayonnaise on white bread, plus energy drinks.
- Dinner: One pound of pasta, an entire pizza, and even more energy drinks.

After retiring for good, Michael changed his diet and ate much healthier, adding tons of fruits and vegetables.

By the time the 2008 Olympics in Beijing, China, arrived, Michael had done everything possible to prepare. He was now twenty-three years old. He knew that this was his chance to do what no one had ever done before: He planned to win eight gold medals in one Olympic Games. Michael and Bob had every moment of that Olympic Games scheduled, down to the minute. Michael knew exactly when he needed to be in the warm-up pool, when to eat, and when to sleep. His schedule was engineered to give him the best chance at winning. After each race, no matter how exciting or emotional, his focus needed to be on the next race.

He won some of the Olympic final races by almost a second or more. These were the 200-meter freestyle, the 800-meter freestyle relay, the 200-meter individual medley, the 400-meter individual medley, and the 400-medley relay. In swimming, a second is a relatively big margin.

Michael even set world records in four of those races.

However, some of the other races were much closer. The 200-meter butterfly was Michael's signature event. It was the same event that got him to the Sydney Olympics eight years earlier. He was the defending champion from the Athens Olympics. It was supposed to be an easy win for him. But when Michael dove into the pool, his goggles filled with water! This had never happened to him before in a big competition. He couldn't see where he was going! Most swimmers would assume they were going to lose the race in that moment. But instead of feeling panicked, Michael felt prepared. He knew exactly how many strokes to take before he would get to the end of the pool. The number of strokes was different on each lap, depending on his speed and tiredness. And Michael had practiced swimming with broken goggles at race pace before, thanks to Bob's training.

Michael won the race!

Before the 4 × 100 freestyle relay began, the French team had been swimming much faster than the Americans had in prior events. The best swimmer on the French team had told reporters that his team would "smash the Americans."

Instead of scaring Michael and his teammates, the "trash talk" motivated them.

Michael swam the first leg of that relay.

Jason Lezak wins the 4 × 100 freestyle relay for Team USA, 2008

When the final swimmers from each team dove in, the French were more than half a body length ahead of the Americans. But in the final meters, Michael's teammate Jason Lezak overcame the French swimmer to win gold! Many swimming fans have called that race the greatest relay of all time.

The closest race, however, was the 100-meter

butterfly. Michael won that race by just 0.01 seconds! He won it by taking a half stroke into the wall. In the end, Michael Phelps became the greatest Olympian of all time. He won eight gold medals in just one Olympics! Many people had said it was impossible, but Michael did it. And his mother and sister were with him in Beijing. They cheered for Michael at every event, and he ran to give them hugs and kisses after he won his eighth gold medal.

Michael took home the $1 million bonus from Speedo and left Beijing as one of the most famous athletes in the world.

CHAPTER 6
Changing Waters

After the excitement of the Beijing Olympics wore off, Michael began to feel lost. He had just become the greatest Olympic athlete in history; now what was left to motivate him? How could he ever match or beat the joy that came from the Beijing Olympics?

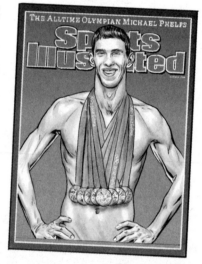

Michael realized he needed a break because swimming wasn't fun for him anymore. His relationship with Bob was getting more difficult, too. In the past, Michael would do anything Bob told him to.

But now, Michael pushed back and argued. He
wanted to make his own choices. He skipped
practices. He kept swimming but not in the old
Michael Phelps way. His head and heart weren't
in it. Other swimmers would overhear Michael
and Bob arguing with each other.

Around 2010 in the middle of a practice, Michael and Bob had their biggest argument yet. Michael didn't show up at practice for ten days after the argument. On the eleventh day, Michael had a big interview with the *Today* show about his preparation for the 2012 Olympics. During the interview, Michael realized he would have to train harder and more consistently if he was going to fulfill his contracts. Bob agreed to start working together again, on one condition. Michael would have to do an intense altitude training trip to get back to his disciplined schedule.

It was back to practice. Michael and Bob traveled to Colorado Springs to train at high altitude for six weeks, working out three times a day. There is less oxygen in the air at high altitude. That makes any physical activity much more difficult. Many athletes go to places like Colorado Springs for training once or twice a year. The longest Michael had trained at high altitude in the past was just three weeks, and that was difficult enough. Training at high altitude for six weeks while out of shape was one of the hardest things Michael had ever done.

U.S. Olympic & Paralympic Training Center in Colorado Springs

After that trip, Michael was back to his previous training schedule, but he wasn't enjoying it like he used to.

At the London Olympics in 2012, Michael knew that he wasn't ready to compete. He barely made the final in the 400-meter individual medley. He ended up finishing fourth in that event. Next, he finished second in his signature 200-meter butterfly to a rival, Chad le Clos of South Africa. Later, Michael would say that he got the results he deserved. He knew Chad had trained harder.

Chad le Clos

Even though Michael ended up winning two silver medals and four gold medals at the games, he made a shocking announcement to the press: He was officially retired. He felt like he never wanted to jump into the pool again.

Sadly, it is common for athletes to become depressed after competing in the Olympics. Being diagnosed with clinical depression means that someone has lost interest in things they used to love. People with depression have extremely low moods and low self-esteem. They may think bad things about themselves. They may have trouble connecting with others and may not have the energy to do daily tasks like eating, brushing their teeth, and showering. Many people who have gone through depression say that it is the most difficult thing they have ever experienced.

For many Olympic athletes, the extreme happiness of participating in the Olympic Games can be followed by struggles to readjust to normal life. That can be even more true after they retire, when they lose the structure that comes with training regularly. Many athletes have trouble knowing who they truly are outside of competing in their sports. Some of them also say sports organizations don't do enough to support their mental health when they are no longer competing.

Throughout his swimming career, Michael struggled with depression. He had many tools to focus on his physical health. But he didn't have the resources he needed for his mental health. The public, and even some of his closest friends and family, didn't know how much he was struggling. He would say later that he only liked himself as a swimmer. He didn't like himself as a person. He didn't know who he was outside the pool.

Sometimes people use alcohol to deal with depression and low self-esteem. Alcohol can make the problems even worse, and it also can lead to bad decisions. Back in 2004, soon after the Athens Olympics, Michael had been arrested for driving under the influence of alcohol. Driving while drunk is incredibly dangerous, which is why it is illegal. Alcohol is especially dangerous for teenagers and young adults. (Michael was nineteen years old at the time.) Michael apologized on television, saying he had "let a lot of people in the country down." He also traveled to high schools and spoke to teenagers about the dangers of drinking alcohol and driving.

Michael would later come to see that incident as a cry for help. Unfortunately, he didn't get the mental-health help he needed. So instead, he put all his focus into swimming. Sometimes his struggles would come out in other ways, though, including other bad decisions. In 2009, a photo of twenty-three-year-old Michael using an illegal drug went viral on the internet. The breaking point for him came in 2014, though, when he was twenty-nine. Michael was two years into his retirement after the London Olympics when he was arrested for the second time for driving under the influence of alcohol. He was in the middle of his worst depression yet.

Michael is arrested in 2014.

He would come to call that day his "rock bottom." After that incident, he reached out for mental-health help. Michael was able to get treatment to help him with his depression. Through the treatment, he learned that he wasn't the only person who dealt with this condition. He learned how to work through his feelings. He also had help learning to build his self-esteem.

Michael reached out to friends and family members, including other Olympic athletes and teammates who had struggled with depression. Connecting with friends, family, and other athletes who had similar experiences helped Michael learn how to talk through his problems. He slowly started to feel better. He learned that he had many people in his life who loved and supported him. He had his friends, his sisters, his parents, and more. Those people all loved him for Michael the person and not just Michael the swimmer.

Michael started to make changes in his life. During treatment, he reconnected with his father. Michael and Fred had had an on-and-off relationship since Fred and Debbie divorced. Though they still weren't close, it was nice to talk with his dad.

Michael made another change to his personal life: He proposed to his girlfriend, Nicole Johnson. He had met Nicole at an award show in 2007, and

Nicole Johnson

they had been dating on and off ever since. Being in treatment helped Michael feel happier than he had been in a very long time. He couldn't see himself being with anyone but Nicole and wanted to let her know he was committed to their relationship. She said yes to his proposal, and they agreed to get married.

During his treatment, Michael began working out again. He was beginning to think maybe he should give his swimming career one more try.

He wanted to regain the structure that swimming brought to his life. He wanted another chance to replay the end of his career, this time with a new outlook on life. He knew that if he wanted to get back in the water he would need Bob by his side, so he reached out to his old friend and coach.

At the time, Bob was worried for Michael and was hesitant to begin working with him again.

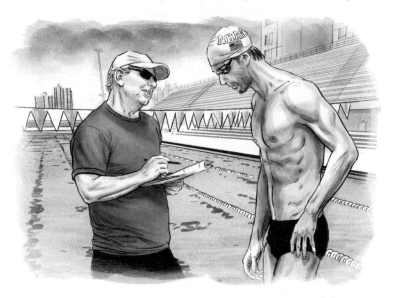

The years leading up to the London Olympics had been miserable for them both. But Michael was able to convince Bob to coach him. Things were going to be different this time. Maybe Michael could return for the Rio de Janeiro 2016 Olympics in Brazil.

CHAPTER 7
A New Man

It was 2015, and the Rio de Janeiro Olympics were around the corner. The news was out—Michael Phelps was making his comeback.

More importantly, Michael had opened up to the world about his struggles with mental health. In an interview with *Sports Illustrated*, he talked about his depression and his recovery.

Michael wanted to compete at this one last Olympics to really enjoy it. He was going to do it his way and show his true self to the world.

But first, in 2016, Michael and Nicole got married and had their first son, Boomer Robert Phelps. After watching Boomer's birth, Michael said that experience was "probably the best thing I've ever, ever been able to be a part of."

He loved being a father and could not wait to share dinners with his wife and son and watch his family grow.

At the training camp before the Olympics, Michael's coaches and teammates had noticed a big change in his personality. In the past, Michael had lived in his own world at big swim meets. He stuck to his schedule and focused only on himself, his races, and his own goals. But this time, Michael connected with his teammates. He joked and shared wisdom with the younger Olympic swimmers. He seemed more relaxed and wanted to get to know everyone on the team.

Michael's coaches and teammates named him team captain for the very first time. He was also selected to be a flag bearer at the 2016

Olympic opening ceremony in Brazil. Michael's new attitude was apparent to his team and to the world watching.

By the time the Summer Olympics rolled around in August, Boomer was old enough to join the rest of the family, cheering Michael on in the stands. Boomer wore big headphones to protect his baby ears.

After winning gold in the 4 × 100-meter freestyle relay, Michael's teammate Ryan Held was overcome with emotion and started crying hard while standing on the podium. Michael put his arm around Ryan, consoling him and telling him it was okay to have these big feelings and that he should appreciate this important moment.

Although Michael's caring and concern for others had grown, his focus and competitive nature remained as strong as ever. In the ready room before the 200-meter butterfly, Michael sat in the corner listening to music quietly to prepare and rest. Chad le Clos of South Africa, who had beaten Michael to the gold medal in 2012, stood near Michael. Chad started shadow boxing, pretending to punch an invisible opponent.

Michael was taken aback! Why would anyone use up their energy doing something so silly? Was Chad trying to intimidate him? Why didn't Chad conserve energy for the race? Cameras caught Michael making a grimacing face at Chad.

The face went viral instantly on the internet, and people used the hashtag #PhelpsFace when posting about the image. People around the world laughed at Michael. He came to joke about the face as well in the future—he knew his intensity in that moment was quite funny!

Michael used his anger with Chad and the media as fuel once again. It was the same lesson he had learned as a child when he decided not to throw his goggles. He would instead channel his emotions into the race. Michael outswam Chad and regained his 200-meter butterfly Olympic title!

Michael's final individual race of his career came in the 100-meter butterfly. He was slow in

Joseph Schooling

the first half, but he got even with the field as the second half came to an end. Twenty-one-year-old Joseph Schooling of Singapore was ahead of the field. If Joseph were to win, he would become the first-ever Olympic gold medalist for his country.

Joseph had grown up idolizing Michael. Michael may not have remembered, but he and Joseph had met in 2008 when Michael was training with the US Olympic team in Singapore. They were in Southeast Asia acclimating to the time zone before the Beijing Olympics. The thirteen-year-old Joseph walked up to Michael and asked him for a photo. The photo shows a young Joseph with braces standing next to Michael Phelps, who was about to become the greatest Olympian in history. Joseph was one of thousands of young people across the world who had been inspired by Michael to swim.

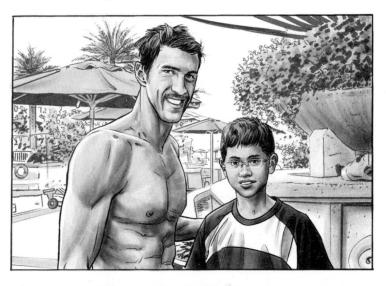

Michael and Joseph Schooling, 2008

At the finish, Joseph hit the wall first. He'd won! Michael finished second, tying for second with two of his longtime competitors.

That race was a fitting end for Michael's swimming career, passing the torch off to the younger generation.

Michael had come into the sport of swimming wanting to change it forever. And he did! Swimming had become more popular in the United States and the world due to what swimming experts call the "Michael Phelps effect."

After every Olympics Michael Phelps swam in, the United States would see more people enroll in swimming classes and join swim clubs and teams.

More and more kids were discovering the joys of swimming, just as Michael had hoped. But since he had become a professional, Michael's goals outside the pool had grown and changed. While he was still focused on teaching kids about water safety, Michael was driven more than ever to help people learn about depression and mental health.

CHAPTER 8
The Next Wave

Michael retired from swimming as the most decorated Olympian of all time. He had won twenty-eight Olympic medals, twenty-three of them gold, over the course of five Olympic

Games. He is often said to be one of the greatest athletes, if not the greatest athlete, of all time.

Michael's second retirement from swimming in 2016 was a new beginning for his life.

In 2008, Michael established the Michael Phelps Foundation as a way to teach water safety to children, using the $1 million sponsorship bonus he received after winning his eighth gold medal. Now that he was retired, Michael spent

most of his time growing the foundation. He expanded the organization's mission to include raising awareness of mental health and depression for adults, something Michael knows about all too well. The foundation also includes programming around teaching children about their emotions and basic mental health skills.

In addition to working with the foundation, Michael also spends his time with Nicole and

their kids. They now have three sons: Boomer, Beckett (born February 12, 2018), and Maverick (born September 9, 2019).

Michael and his family live in Arizona, not too far from where Bob coaches the Arizona State swim team. Michael and his former coach remain close. Michael volunteers as an assistant coach to the team, and Bob acts like a grandparent to Michael's children.

In 2020, Michael executive produced and narrated *The Weight of Gold*, a documentary about the mental health struggles Olympic athletes face before, during, and after the games. The film showed Michael and other Olympic athletes talking about the overwhelming feelings they experience because every part of their lives is focused only on making it to, and winning at, the Olympics.

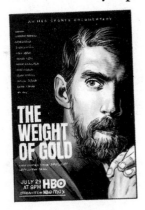

Michael has said that one of his biggest goals is to help reduce rates of depression in the United States both among elite athletes and the general public. He partnered with an online talk-therapy company, and he spreads the message that there is no shame is needing or wanting to talk with a professional about your emotions.

Michael has changed the sport of swimming forever, but he hopes to make a bigger impact on the world through his work in water safety and through his mental health advocacy. He is considered the greatest Olympian and the greatest swimmer of all time, and his legacy in this sport will live on through the next generation of swimmers he inspires.

Timeline of Michael Phelps's Life

1985 — Michael Fred Phelps II is born on June 30 in Baltimore, Maryland

1992 — Starts swimming to join his older sisters' team

1997 — Begins training with swim coach Bob Bowman

2000 — Competes in his first Olympic Games in Sydney, Australia

2001 — Becomes a professional swimmer and signs his first individual endorsement deal with Speedo

2004 — Tries to beat Mark Spitz's record of winning the most gold medals (seven) in one Olympic Games, but he only wins six gold medals and two bronze in Athens, Greece

2008 — Surpasses Spitz's Olympic record by winning eight gold medals at the Olympics in Beijing, China

— Establishes foundation that promotes healthy and active lives, especially for children

2012 — Announces his retirement at the London Olympics

2014 — Begins receiving treatment for his depression, a condition he has struggled with his whole life

2015 — Comes out of retirement for the 2016 Olympic Games

2016 — Becomes the most decorated Olympian in the world after winning six medals at the Rio de Janeiro Olympics

— Retires from professional swimming for the last time

Timeline of the World

1986 — US space shuttle *Challenger* explodes after it launches at Cape Canaveral, Florida

1989 — Nintendo company releases the Game Boy in Japan in April and in North America in July

1992 — The Mall of America, the largest shopping mall in the United States, opens in Bloomington, Minnesota

1997 — Diana, Princess of Wales, dies in a car crash in Paris, France

— Tiger Woods, age twenty-one, becomes the youngest-ever golfer to win the Masters

2004 — The Boston Red Sox baseball team wins the World Series for the first time since 1918

2005 — The video-sharing website YouTube is founded

2010 — The Burj Khalifa skyscraper in Dubai opens and becomes the tallest building in the world

2015 — Queen Elizabeth II becomes the longest reigning monarch in the history of the United Kingdom

2019 — Swedish environmental activist Greta Thunberg becomes the youngest individual selected as *TIME* magazine's person of the year

2020 — The World Health Organization declares COVID-19— a potentially deadly disease—a global pandemic

Bibliography

*Books for young readers

Bowmile, Mitch. "Michael Phelps: The Making of a Champion." *SwimSwam Magazine*, May 8, 2020. https://swimswam.com/michael-phelps-the-making-of-a-champion/.

*Fishman, Jon M. *Michael Phelps*. Minneapolis, MN: Lerner Publications, 2017.

Michael Phelps: Medals, Memories, and More. Season 1. Peacock Originals, 2020.

Phelps, Michael, with Brian Cazeneuve. *Michael Phelps: Beneath the Surface*. Champaign, IL: Sports Publishing, 2016.

Phelps, Michael, with Alan Abrahamson. *No Limits: The Will to Succeed*. New York: Free Press, 2009.

Rapkin, Brett, dir. *The Weight of Gold*. 2020. Bel Air, CA: Podium Pictures.

YOUR HEADQUARTERS FOR HISTORY

Activities, Mad Libs, and sidesplitting jokes!
Discover the Who HQ books beyond the biographies

Who? What? Where?

Learn more at whohq.com!